WELCOME TO ST ANDREWS

Now a picturesque seaside town, famous for its golf and its university, St Andrews was once Scotland's premier cathedral city. Throughout the Middle Ages, it was the centre of the Scottish Church. The great cathedral dominated a wealthy ecclesiastical burgh, whose street plan survives much as it was 500 years ago.

The buildings erected here were on a scale of magnificence unequalled elsewhere in Scotland. Fortunately many of them survive as a testament to the wealth and influence of the Church, personified in the bishops and archbishops who resided at the castle.

Some of the most important events in Scotland's history have taken place here. The cathedral bears witness to the pious ambitions of generations of patrons; while kings, nobles, martyrs and reformers have all dwelt within the castle walls. The history of both buildings intertwines with that of the burgh – a story that is sometimes turbulent, sometimes glorious and often dramatic. The town named for Scotland's patron saint has retained its iconic status for nearly 1,000 years.

CONTENTS

Opposite: Inside the mine dug during the siege of the castle in 1546–7.

HIGHLIGHTS

St Andrews Castle and Cathedral are situated a few hundred metres apart, close to the town's craggy north-eastern coastline. Other historic landmarks are dispersed around the centre of the town. We recommend you do not miss these highlights.

THE CASTLE

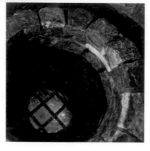

▲ BOTTLE DUNGEON
Few medieval dungeons are grimmer than this pit hollowed out from the rock, where the lowliest prisoners endured miserable conditions (p.16).

▲ THE MINE AND COUNTERMINE
An extraordinary relic of the siege of 1546–7, when government forces attempted to tunnel under the castle but were intercepted by the besieged rebels (p.18).

◄ THE HAMILTON FAÇADE
The prestigious entrance front added by Archbishop John Hamilton around 1550 announces his importance and the prestige associated with his castle (p.9).

THE HISTORIC BURGH

◄ ST SALVATOR'S COLLEGE
The earliest of the university's three medieval colleges, St Salvator's retains its impressive medieval chapel and tower (p.46).

◄ THE WEST PORT
A gate into the walled burgh, built in 1587 and incorporating the fabric of an earlier port. It was remodelled in Victorian times (p.45).

◀ A GREAT BUILDING PROJECT

As Scotland's most important church, St Andrews Cathedral was designed to be overwhelmingly vast and grand, but these aspirations were not achieved without setbacks (p.54).

THE CATHEDRAL MUSEUM ▶

Home to a host of carved stones drawn from many periods of the cathedral's history, from the Pictish St Andrews Sarcophagus to elaborately carved gravestones from the 1600s (p.35).

◀ THE VIEW FROM ST RULE'S TOWER

The long climb up a spiral staircase is rewarded with a superb panorama over the historic burgh and the coastline (p.24).

◀ THE EAST GABLE

The most complete part of the cathedral still standing. Viewed from the west entrance, it conveys a sense of the medieval building's scale and magnificence (p.30).

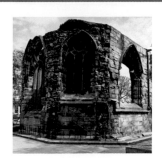

◀ BLACKFRIARS CHAPEL

A small, ruined chapel is all that remains of the Dominican friary that co-existed with the Augustinian cathedral priory (p.45).

◀ A SPORTING REVIVAL

After the Reformation, St Andrews was revitalised by golf, which has made the town an international focus for sport (p.71).

ST ANDREWS CASTLE

St Andrews Castle was the chief residence of the bishops, and later the archbishops, of St Andrews. They were Scotland's leading churchmen, and lived in a manner reflecting their exalted status. They also had to be prepared to defend themselves and the property of the Church – hence their strong castle.

During its 450-year history, St Andrews Castle served as episcopal palace, fortress and state prison. It was also the setting for many important events, not all of them hosted by the prelate. James I held a great Christmas pageant here in 1425, and his grandson, James III, may well have been born in the castle in 1452. Great people from home and abroad were richly housed and lavishly entertained within its walls; others less fortunate were confined in its grim dungeons.

ST ANDREWS CASTLE AT A GLANCE

The castle stands on a headland projecting into St Andrews Bay. Steep cliffs protected it along the north and east sides, and a great ditch cut through the solid bedrock defined the defensive circuit on the landward side to south and west. Little of the original 12th and 13th-century castle remains. More survives of the castle as rebuilt by Bishop Traill around 1390, most obviously the lofty fore tower. Much of what we see today dates from the 16th century.

1 SITE OF OUTER COURTYARD

The visitor centre now stands in what was once an outer service court, housing stables, workshops and possibly a bakehouse and brewhouse.

2 FORE TOWER

The imposing tower through which the castle's ground-floor entrance originally passed. It now stands four storeys high. The entrance was moved to its present position in the 1500s.

3 ENTRANCE FRONT

The impressive new entrance front was added by Archbishop Hamilton after the great siege of 1546–7.

4 INNER COURTYARD

This spacious court would once have been cobbled and surrounded on all sides by impressive buildings. The main feature now surviving is the well.

5 SOUTH RANGE

Created as a state apartment for Archbishop Hamilton following the 1546–7 siege, and originally reached via a stone forestair at the east end.

6 SITE OF CHAPEL RANGE

Little survives of this part of the south range, but we know that it held a chapel on its first floor and featured a loggia, or covered open arcade, facing the courtyard.

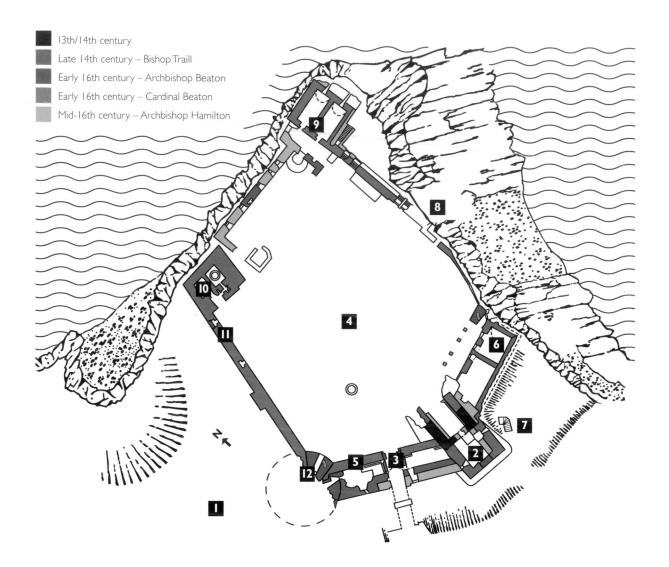

13th/14th century

Late 14th century – Bishop Traill

Early 16th century – Archbishop Beaton

Early 16th century – Cardinal Beaton

Mid-16th century – Archbishop Hamilton

7 MINE AND COUNTERMINE

A fascinating remnant of the siege of 1546–7, dug by the attackers and the desperate defenders respectively. These are among the most important medieval siege works to be found anywhere in Europe.

8 SITE OF GREAT HALL

A large, splendidly decorated reception room, serviced by the kitchen immediately to its north. It was swept away by a storm in 1801.

9 KITCHEN TOWER AND SEA GATE

The castle's main kitchen survives on the first floor, with vaulted storage cellars below.

10 SEA TOWER AND BOTTLE DUNGEON

Rebuilt by Bishop Traill in the late 1300s, the sea tower may always have been intended to house prisoners of varying status. The humblest prisoners were confined to the grim 'bottle dungeon' in its basement.

11 SITE OF POSTERN

The service entrance to the castle complex, used by servants, workmen and the like. Blocked up in the 1520s or 30s.

12 BLOCKHOUSE RUINS

One of two gun towers added in the 1520s or 30s at the SE and SW corners of the inner courtyard. Little remains of the other.

ENTRANCES TO THE CASTLE

The south side of the castle, facing the town, housed the front entrance. It was always intended to impress. The imposing fore tower housed that entrance for much of the castle's life. During the 1500s, this was blocked up and replaced by the present entrance to its west.

THE FORE TOWER

This is one of the oldest parts of the castle ruin, with 12th or 13th-century masonry embedded in its lowest courses. However, much of what we see dates from Bishop Traill's time (1385–1401).

The tower housed the castle's original main entrance. Although subsequently blocked up, the sides of the gateway have been partly exposed (below the lowest window). The gateway was protected by a portcullis and two-leafed door. High above the gateway, to the right of the second window up, is a narrow vertical slot. This was one of two slots that held the 'gaffs' or beams that raised and lowered the drawbridge (see illustration, page 58). Such drawbridges are rare: only three others are known in Scotland – at Bothwell, Dalhousie and Linlithgow Palace. Like St Andrews, they all date from around 1400.

When the castle's entrance was relocated to its present position, the fore tower gateway was blocked up. The battered (sloping) masonry at the tower's base was added to strengthen the walls against undermining. The entrance passage and the room above it (which housed the mechanisms for operating the drawbridge and portcullis) were made into rooms; hence the windows. We do not know when these alterations were made. The square armorial panel between the two large windows would have told us more had it not weathered beyond legibility, but a date in the early 1500s seems most likely.

THE ENTRANCE FRONT

The present impressive entrance front was built in the time of Archbishop Hamilton (1546–71). Directly above the entrance gateway is a framed panel that once held a coat of arms. The date 1555, now barely visible, is carved on a stone below it. Above the panel runs a frieze of four roundels, each with a cinquefoil (five-petalled flower) – Hamilton's armorial badge. The small door to the right of the entrance served as pedestrian access when the main doors were closed.

Most of the rest of the entrance front is Archbishop Hamilton's too. Although fragmentary, it retains enough to show that it was a most impressive piece of early Scottish classicism. The ranges flanking the entrance had symmetrical windows at first-floor level. There is evidence for fine dormer windows lighting the top storey: their ornate stepped sills can be seen at the present wall-head. An engraving made by John Slezer around 1690 (see page 70), shows the entrance front when more complete. Down and to the left of the entrance, tucked into the corner just above the grass, are the remains of a wide-throated gunhole from one of two blockhouses added by Archbishop James Beaton in the 1520s (see page 19).

Left: One of the cinquefoils on the frieze above the entrance. This floral motif was Archbishop Hamilton's armorial badge.

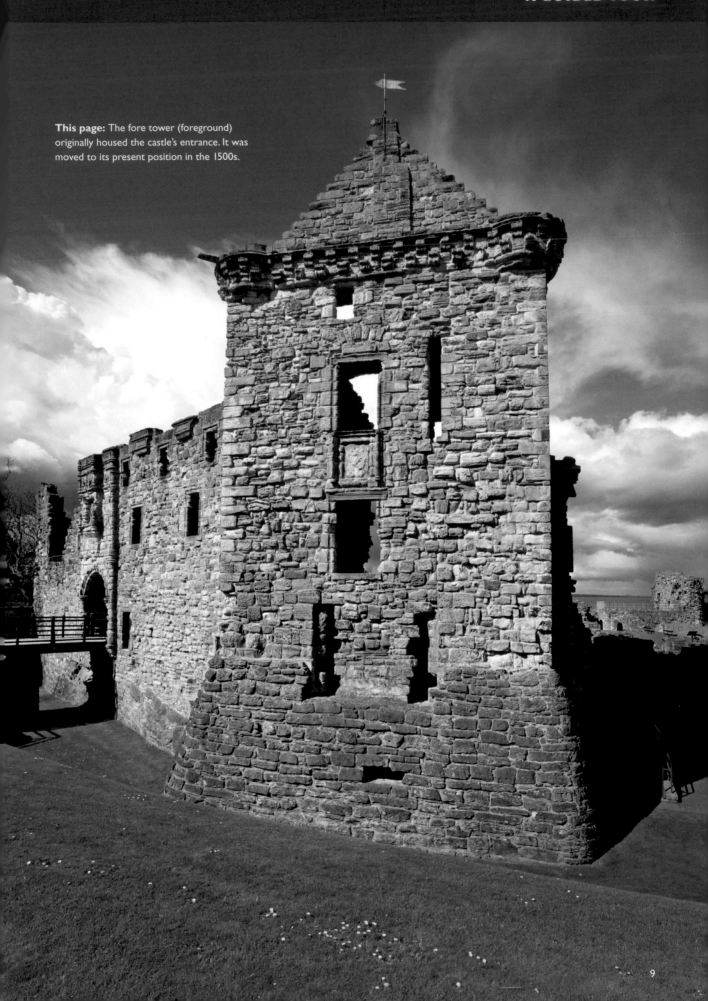

This page: The fore tower (foreground) originally housed the castle's entrance. It was moved to its present position in the 1500s.

THE CASTLE INTERIOR

The castle courtyard was the domain of the lord-bishops. The buildings and towers ranged around its four sides housed residential accommodation and service offices for them, their senior household (constable, steward, etc), guests – and prisoners.

THE ENTRANCE PEND

The present entrance passage and the gloomy vaults to either side date from after 1550. Prior to then, this area was open space, and outside the castle's south curtain wall.

The vaulted pend has long guard-chambers on either side. Each has a vertical shaft, cut down through the rock by the defending garrison during the 1546–7 siege – failed attempts to locate the enemy's mine (see page 16). The end wall of the east chamber clearly shows the junction between the original fore tower and its later extension to the south.

The end wall of the west chamber is part of the outer curved wall of the 1520s blockhouse; the splayed opening in it was the gunhole that defended the original curtain wall to its right. This wall has a splayed plinth near the base, indicating that it was once an outside wall. The date when the present inner entrance was formed through that curtain wall is not clear. It may have been as late as the 1520s, part of the same building programme that resulted in the two blockhouses.

THE INNER COURTYARD AND WELL

Archaeologists excavating the site of the visitor centre in 1989 discovered an outer courtyard housing service buildings (bakehouse, brewhouse, etc). This inner courtyard served as a *cour d'honneur* (court of honour), reserved for the bishop's ceremonial use. It was once paved. The only feature visible today is the well.

THE SOUTH RANGE

The two floors above the front entrance were created by Archbishop Hamilton in the 1550s to serve as his state apartment (hall and private chambers). The state rooms of his predecessors, on the east side of the fore tower, had been extensively damaged in the 1546–7 siege; hence their relocation. The first floor housed Hamilton's hall and was reached via a stone forestair at the east end, beside the fore tower. (The floor is now reached by a later spiral stair at the west end.) The ruinous state of the range forbids a more detailed layout of the archbishop's accommodation.

Opposite top: The castle courtyard as viewed from the south range.

Opposite bottom left: The entrance pend, with the kitchen tower beyond.

Top left: The east guard-chamber flanking the pend.

Bottom left: The state apartment of Archbishop Hamilton, above the present entrance.

INSIDE THE FORE TOWER

The tower housing the main entrance was extended outwards and upwards in the late 1300s, and its gate was blocked in the early 1500s when the present entrance was installed. The fore tower still contains some of the earliest surviving stonework in the castle.

The tower has a complex building history. The lowest courses of masonry in its northern half, nearest the courtyard, are built of large, well-dressed stones, laid in courses with narrow joints, and may belong to the original 12th-century castle. The wall dividing the basement into two compartments incorporates the original entrance gateway, now considerably narrowed by later blocking.

In the early 1300s, the tower was extended to the south and doubled in size. The east wall still retains its postern gate, shrunk into a window in the 1500s. Embedded deep down in the SW corner is an arrow-slit dating from the late 1200s or early 1300s. Bishop Lamberton (1297–1328) is reported to have carried out major building work after Bannockburn in 1314 and this extension may well be his doing.

The fore tower was later heightened, and a new entrance doorway was formed, with an elaborate drawbridge through the south wall. These alterations are attributed to Bishop Traill (1385–1401). When the main entrance was relocated to the south curtain wall in the 1500s, the interior of the tower was converted to ancillary accommodation.

THE EARLIEST BISHOP'S CASTLE

There was probably a bishop's castle from the outset in the 12th century. Archaeological excavations on the site of the visitor centre in 1989 revealed a stone marked 'Robertus' – possibly for Bishop Robert (1123–59) – lending weight to this theory. The presence of masonry from the late 1100s in the fore tower suggests that Bishop Roger de Beaumont (1189–1202) was carrying out building work. As a son of the Earl of Leicester and a cousin of King William the Lion, he would certainly have been familiar with the latest ideas in castle design.

Opposite: The interior of the fore tower. Some of its fabric may date from the 1100s, but repeated alterations have obscured its building history.

Above: The word 'Robertus' is clearly inscribed on this stone, suggesting that the castle may have been started by Bishop Robert (1123–59).

EAST OF THE FORE TOWER

The eastern part of the castle is mostly in poor repair, the result of storms and coastal erosion as much as warfare. However, we know that this area once housed some of the castle's finest buildings.

THE CHAPEL

The south range running east from the fore tower housed the castle chapel on its upper floor. Little of it survives apart from a side of one window, but this fragment, coupled with the evidence from Slezer's engraving (see page 70), shows that the chapel was lit from the south by large, traceried windows dating from the early 1500s. The ground floor of the range had two vaulted chambers set behind a five-bay loggia, or covered open arcade, of which only the bases remain.

Above: The loggia and above it the chapel as they may have looked when complete. Very little survives beyond a fragment of chapel window and the stumps of the loggia pillars.

THE EAST RANGE

On the east side of the range is a fragment of stairwell that once gave access to the east range. This was housed in a tower projecting from the SE corner of the courtyard, which has long since vanished into the sea.

This range housed the castle's most important and prestigious accommodation – the bishops' private apartment and their great banqueting hall. Little other than the west (courtyard) wall now remains. The building was extensively damaged by artillery during the 1546–7 siege, and abandoned in favour of Archbishop Hamilton's new state apartment in the south range. The public entrance to the great hall was towards the north end (that is, at the opposite end from the bishops' apartment) and is marked by the masonry stub of its forestair. There were cavernous storage cellars beneath the great hall.

The loss of this great hall, which finally fell into the sea in 1801, is very regrettable, for it must have rivalled those at Linlithgow Palace and Stirling Castle in scale and splendour.

THE KITCHEN TOWER AND SEA GATE

The kitchen producing banquets for the great hall was on the first floor of the tower at the NE corner of the castle. Only the east wall survives, partly because it was buttressed in the 1500s. It contains a slop-sink and two aumbries (wall cupboards). The kitchen may well have had more than one huge fireplace, like its contemporary at Dirleton Castle in East Lothian. Below the kitchen are two vaulted storage cellars. In the adjacent north range is a circular bread oven.

Between the kitchen tower and the north range is a vaulted pend that leads to the sea gate opening north onto St Andrews Bay. Servants provisioning the castle from the sea would have used this precipitous back entrance.

Above left: The kitchen tower which once served a great banqueting hall in the east range.

Above centre: An aumbry or wall cupboard in the kitchen tower's surviving east wall.

Above right: The sea gate, once used for bringing supplies into the castle.

THE SEA TOWER AND BOTTLE DUNGEON

The sea tower at the NW corner of the courtyard may have served as prison accommodation throughout the castle's active life.

On the ground floor are two chambers. The eastern one was an unlit prison cell, with just a narrow ventilation slit in the east wall. In the floor is the circular opening into the infamous rock cut bottle dungeon, so-called because of its shape. Measuring 7.3m deep and widening to around 4.6m wide at the bottom, this has to be one of the grimmest of Scotland's many grim castle pits, or dungeons. John Knox wrote that: 'In this place, many of God's children were imprisoned.' Among them was the Protestant preacher, George Wishart, in 1546.

The upper floors were devastated by artillery in the 1546–7 siege, when French gunners 'schote doune all the battelyne and caiphouse of the scytoure'. Little can now be said about how they were used. However, a high-status function is indicated by the remains of a fine fireplace in the north wall and a projecting spiral stair leading to the missing upper floor, caphouse and battlements.

The prison at St Andrews held all ranks of prisoner, from the senior aristocracy down to common criminals. This upper floor may have been where the former were 'close-warded'.

Beside the sea tower, in the adjacent west courtyard wall, is a blocked-up postern. This side-entrance was used by servants and workmen passing between the inner and outer courtyards.

Above: A cutaway illustration of the sea tower as it may have looked when complete, showing the three-tiered arrangement of accommodation for prisoners.

THE BLOCKHOUSE

In the SW corner of the courtyard are the remains of a circular blockhouse, or gun-tower. This was one of two, added at either end of the south curtain wall, probably in the 1520s, to improve the castle's defences against gunpowdered artillery. The other, at the SE corner, has long since collapsed into the sea.

These blockhouses replaced the rectangular corner towers of Bishop Traill's castle. They were among the largest in Scotland, with an overall diameter of almost 8m and walls over 2m thick. They stood at least three floors high, but were both extensively damaged during the siege of 1546–7.

If you go through the gate leading back to the visitor centre, then look to your left, you can see the gunhole pointing into the west guard-chamber, covering the inner gate. But remember, when the blockhouse was built, that now dark space was open to the sky.

Left: The ruined sea tower as it looks today.

Below left: Vestigial remains of what was once a fine fireplace show that there was once a comfortable chamber on the first floor. The fireplace dates from the 1200s, indicating that the sea tower is one of the oldest parts of the present castle.

Below: A prisoner's-eye view from inside the bottle dungeon.

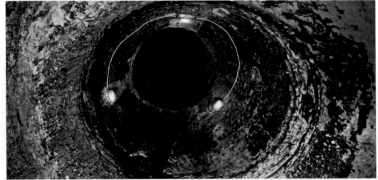

DID YOU KNOW...

After Cardinal Beaton's assassination in 1546 (see page 66) his body was flung into the bottle dungeon. It lay there for many months, preserved in salt to 'keap him frome styncking'.

THE MINE AND COUNTERMINE

Beyond the east range is the entrance to the mine and countermine, fascinating evidence of the ingenuity of 16th-century siege engineering. Visitors who are fit – and not overly prone to claustrophobia – can explore the two contrasting tunnels.

In 1546, St Andrews Castle was under siege, following the dramatic murder of Cardinal Beaton. His assassins, led by a group of Fife lairds, had occupied the castle, and Regent Arran ordered his troops to capture them and regain control. The siege was to last more than a year.

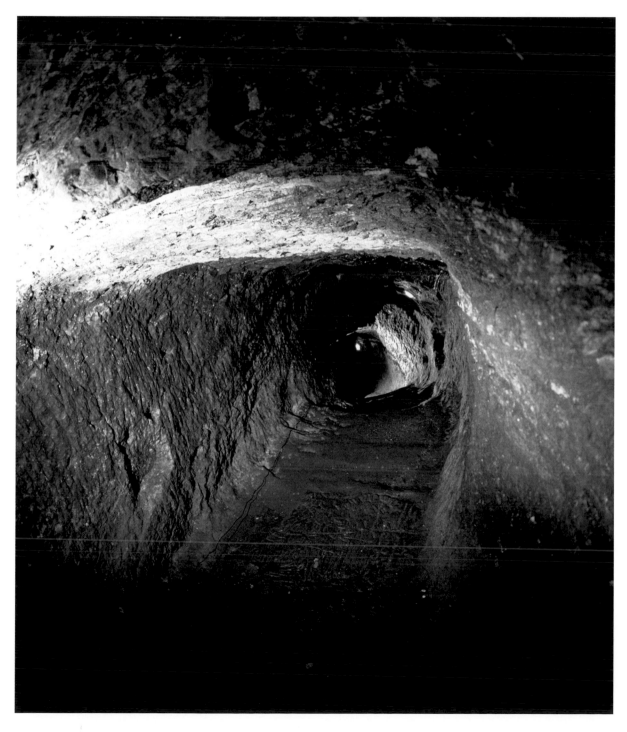

In November 1546, the French ambassador in London, Odet de Selve, reported that the besiegers were digging a mine beneath the castle walls in an attempt to undermine the fore tower. He also reported that the defenders were counter-mining to forestall that attempt.

The mine itself is a spacious stepped corridor, high and wide enough for pack animals to be used for the removal of rock (see inside front cover). The start of the miners' operation would have been visible from the castle battlements – the entrance was within 30m of the castle walls. However, the only clues the defenders had as to the route of the mine were the position of its entrance and the sound of underground digging.

Left: The cramped tunnel built by the desperate counterminers is in stark contrast to the spacious passage of the mine.

Above: When the countermine finally broke through, the mine had reached more than halfway to the fore tower. However, the counterminers were able to repel the besiegers.

There were two unsuccessful attempts to intercept the mine. Digging through solid rock, the defenders began two shafts to the west of the fore tower. These can still be seen in the chambers on either side of the entrance pend. They were eventually abandoned and a third shaft was opened east of the fore tower.

Even on their third attempt, the counterminers had difficulty in locating the mine. The first gallery swung too far to the east and the tunnel was re-routed to the SW. The defenders' desperation is evident in the cramped scale of the gallery they dug, much less spacious than the mine they hoped to intercept. However, they eventually broke through into the mine and the besiegers were repelled.

The mine and countermine still bear the pick marks made by the sappers. After the siege, both were in-filled to prevent re-use. They were only rediscovered in 1879, when the foundations of a new house were being dug. The entrance to the mine can still be seen on the far side of the public road, marked by a circular manhole cover.

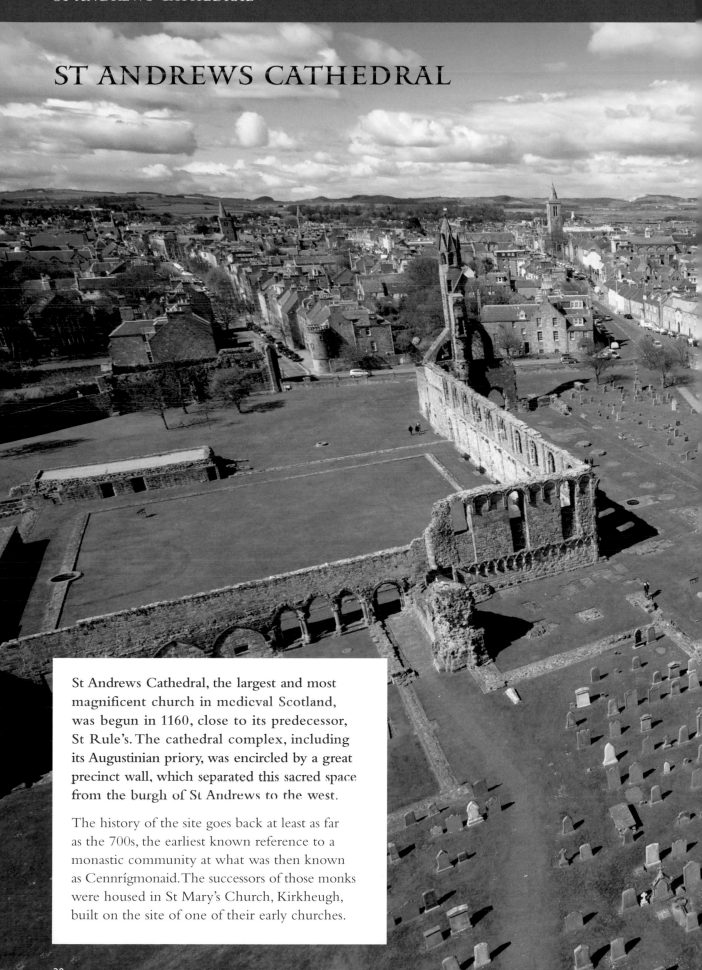

ST ANDREWS CATHEDRAL

St Andrews Cathedral, the largest and most magnificent church in medieval Scotland, was begun in 1160, close to its predecessor, St Rule's. The cathedral complex, including its Augustinian priory, was encircled by a great precinct wall, which separated this sacred space from the burgh of St Andrews to the west.

The history of the site goes back at least as far as the 700s, the earliest known reference to a monastic community at what was then known as Cennrígmonaid. The successors of those monks were housed in St Mary's Church, Kirkheugh, built on the site of one of their early churches.

ST ANDREWS CATHEDRAL AT A GLANCE

The cathedral is sited on a headland to the east of the town. It was begun about 1160 and took well over a century to complete. Severe damage was inflicted by a storm in the 1270s and again by a fire in 1378. Another storm brought down much of the south transept in 1409.

In 1559, a fiery sermon preached by John Knox in the town's parish church aroused the congregation so much that they attacked the cathedral and tore down its rich furnishings. The office of bishop was finally abolished in 1689/90. Deprived of any function, the cathedral fell into ruin. What survives dates mainly from the 1300s and 1400s.

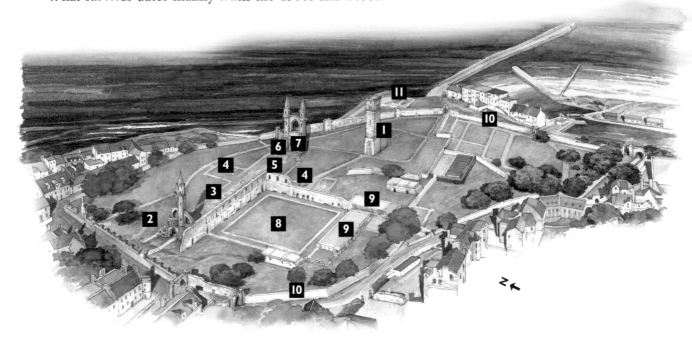

I ST RULE'S CHURCH
The oldest building standing in the town. The lofty tower of St Andrews' first cathedral stands 30m (100ft) high, to the SE of its successor.

2 WEST ENTRANCE
The processional doorway through the impressive west façade would only have been used on feast-days and other special occasions.

3 NAVE
The western part of the church, where lay people worshipped. The missing walls and bare stonework do little justice to what would have been a complex and beautiful space, crammed with altars. Screens would have been used to demarcate chapels in the aisles.

4 TRANSEPTS
The arms of the church to north and south, forming a cross shape. These would also have accommodated additional altars.

5 CHOIR
The eastern part of the church, used during services by the cathedral clergy, separated from the nave by a great rood screen.

6 PRESBYTERY
A raised area at the east end of the church where the high altar stood. The most prestigious burials were here, including Bishop Henry Wardlaw, founder of St Andrews University.

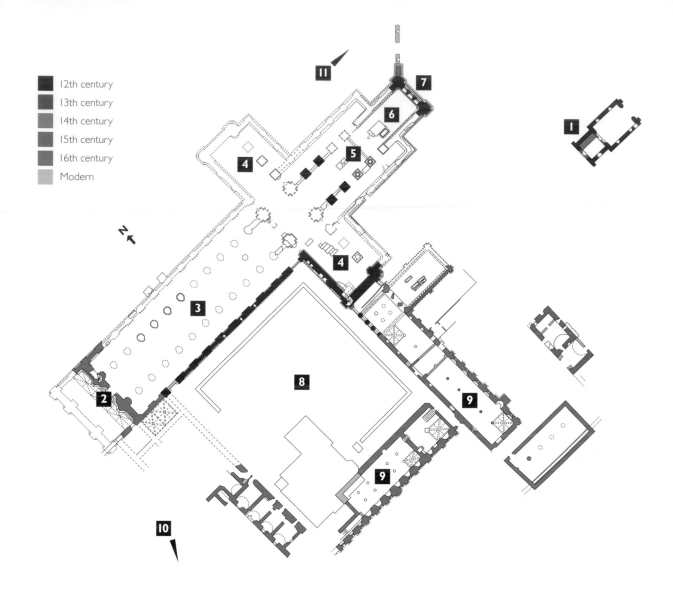

12th century
13th century
14th century
15th century
16th century
Modern

7 RELIC CHAPEL OF ST ANDREW

The chapel housed a shrine believed to contain
relics of the saint. According to legend, they were
brought here by St Rule in AD 345.

8 THE CATHEDRAL PRIORY

Little remains now of the complex built for the
Augustinian canons who served the cathedral.
The chapter house ruins and refectory undercroft
are still impressive.

9 CATHEDRAL MUSEUM

Housed in restored sections of the east and
south ranges, the museum holds an important
collection of medieval carved stones, including
the 8th-century St Andrews Sarcophagus.

10 PRECINCT WALL AND PENDS GATE

Now the most complete precinct wall in Scotland,
it once enclosed the entire sprawling cathedral
complex. The splendid Pends Gate SW of the
cathedral survives almost complete.

11 ST MARY'S CHURCH, KIRKHEUGH

Outside the precinct wall, on a promontory
overlooking the harbour, are the remains of
St Mary's Church (known as St Mary's on
the Rock). This was where the successors
of the Celtic monks were housed in the
later Middle Ages.

ST RULE'S

St Rule's Church appears to have been the first cathedral building at St Andrews. It probably dates from the time of Robert, Prior of Scone, brought to St Andrews by King Alexander I in 1123.

The dating of St Rule's is one of the great problems of Scottish architectural history. Some would like to see it as a pre-12th century church, dating to the time of Fothad, bishop of Cennrígmonaid (1059–93), who married Malcolm III to Queen Margaret at Dunfermline around 1070. However, most of the architecture of St Rule's appears to date from after 1123, during Bishop Robert's time. Robert was the prior of the first Augustinian foundation in Scotland, at Scone in Perthshire.

St Rule's originally consisted of a tall tower with a rectangular chancel to its east and perhaps a semi-circular apse beyond. The tower, over 100ft (30m) high, would have served as a beacon for pilgrims heading for the shrine of St Andrew. Before the church was extended in the 1140s, the tower stood at the west end. It was linked to the chancel by a high arch (now blocked). Scars on the tower's east face record changes to the chancel's roof.

Around 1144, another compartment was added east of the chancel, and a nave added west of the tower. Both have since been demolished, but the elaborate arches cut through the east end of the chancel and the west side of the tower indicate their former existence.

By the time St Rule's was extended in 1144, Bishop Robert was confident enough to introduce a chapter of Augustinian canons into what had been a pre-eminent centre of Celtic spirituality. This was the latest of several attempts to reform the church at St Andrews and supplant the existing Culdee clergy. St Rule's marks his success in doing so. It is likely that there were earlier buildings alongside the church which housed the canons, although these no longer remain.

Top left: Inside St Rule's tower.

Top: St Rule's tower viewed from within the surviving chancel. The evidence of at least three different roofs indicates that the church was repeatedly altered.

St Rule's continued to be used and modified after the new cathedral was built in the 1160s. The doorway on the east wall has the arms of Prior John Hepburn (1483–1526) above it. Around Hepburn's time, the tower was heightened by a few courses, perhaps to provide a firm base for a timber spire.

The present doorway through the west arch dates to the 1500s. The stone spiral stair was probably inserted into the upper part of the tower at this time.

For a bird's-eye view of the cathedral and town, enter the tower and climb the steep, narrow, spiral staircase to the top. This is the best place to appreciate the scale of the cathedral.

Left: St Rule's Church as it may have looked around 1150, a few years before building work began on the great cathedral.

THE CATHEDRAL

St Rule's Church soon proved too small for the community of Augustinian canons. Work began on a much grander cathedral, which became the focus of the newly founded ecclesiastical burgh of St Andrews.

The new cathedral was begun around 1160 by Bishop Arnold. Construction began at the east end. This was the most important part of the church, where the choir and the high altar were situated. Construction took many years.

In 1202 Bishop Roger Beaumont had to be buried in St Rule's because the new cathedral was still not ready to receive his body. His successor, Bishop Malvoisin, was the first to be buried at the cathedral, in 1238.

With the east end completed, the builders moved onto the nave to its west. This was nearly complete by the 1270s, during Bishop Wishart's time. The mortar had barely set when a great gale blew down the west front in 1272.

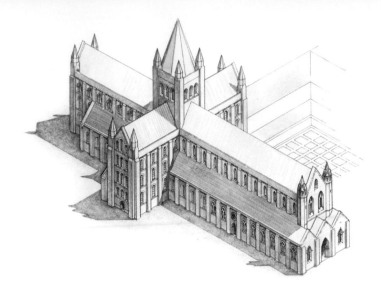

Below left: The surviving towers and walls of the cathedral still convey an impression of its scale and grandeur.

Left: The cathedral as it may have looked when complete, towards the end of the 13th century.

Below: A carved stone head of Christ, one of many embellishments which would once have adorned the cathedral, now displayed in the on-site museum.

A new west front was built a little further east, shortening the cathedral. A porch was added to the west front and this remained in place until the 14th century. At 140m in length, St Andrews Cathedral would have been the longest church in Scotland, almost on a par with the major cathedrals of England such as York (158m) and Durham (150m). However, two bays collapsed in the 1270s, reducing the length to 109m.

The outbreak of the Wars of Independence with England in 1296 prevented the consecration of the completed cathedral until 5 July 1318, four years after King Robert Bruce's great victory at Bannockburn. It was carried out with great ceremony and in the presence of the king himself.

St Andrews Cathedral is a landmark in the transition from Romanesque architecture, with its solid, semi-circular arches, barrel vaults and thick walls, to the slender, pointed features of Gothic architecture. The transition between the two styles can be followed from east to west in the surviving nave wall. It was influential in passing on some of the new ideas which had been introduced into northern England by the Cistercian monks of eastern France. Many features of its design seem to have provided inspiration for monastic churches elsewhere in Scotland – at Jedburgh and Arbroath, for example – and in northern England, at Hexham and Lanercost.

THE WEST FRONT AND NAVE

The great processional entrance at the centre of the west front was only used on high days and holy days. It was intended to impress and overawe, and it still does.

The magnificent doorway, with its five receding arches, was flanked by tall turrets on either side. A stone vaulted porch stretched right across the west front and up to the height of the nave aisles. Although this has now gone, the lines of the vaulting ribs are still visible.

The upper part of the west front was rebuilt after a great fire in 1378. Two tiers of windows were inserted above a row of decorative blind arches and handsome pinnacles were added to the turrets. The porch was probably removed at the same time. The new windows, of which only one survives, suggest some French architectural influence. It is not known which bishop paid for them, but

Bishop Landallis (died 1385) had been appointed at the request of the French king, and Bishop Traill (died 1410) was educated at the University of Paris. Both knew France well enough to have introduced the idea.

There were several entrances into the cathedral besides the western door. Lay people normally entered through a door halfway along the north side of the nave. This was eventually sheltered by a porch. The doorways along the south side of the church led from the cloister into the church and were for the exclusive use of the canons.

Through the west door was the nave, where lay people gathered for worship. It eventually came to house a large number of side altars, some of them chantry chapels, where priests would pray for the souls of individuals or members of merchant and craft guilds in the burgh.

The nave was originally designed to have 14 bays, but this was reduced to 12 following the collapse of the west front in the 1270s. There is evidence for this in the SW corner, where a portion of later masonry has been removed to expose the original south wall. The eastern part of the nave was built at the same time as the choir, to provide support for a massive central bell-tower which once stood over the crossing. The rest of the nave was only nearing completion in the 1270s, after almost a century of building.

During the protracted course of these works, architectural fashions changed. Evidence of this can be detected in the surviving south wall of the nave. The most obvious change is in the design of the windows, which pass from the simple round-headed form at the east end to the pointed arches with Y-shaped bars at the west end.

Left: The west façade as it may have looked following rebuilding after the fire in 1378.

Opposite: The west façade as it looks now.

Opposite (inset): A doorway (now blocked) leading from the nave into the priory cloister.

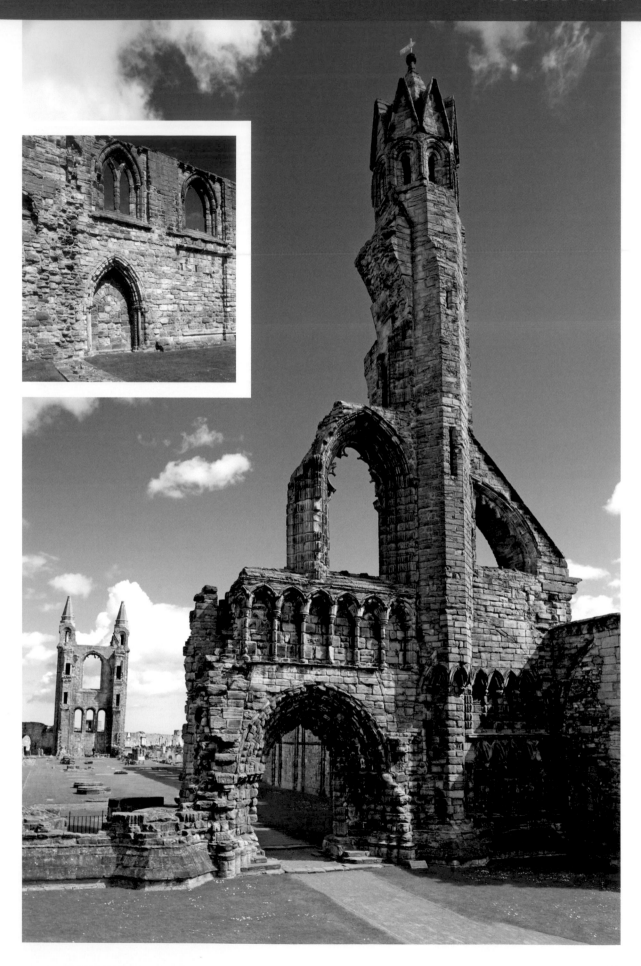

THE TRANSEPTS, CHOIR AND PRESBYTERY

The cathedral was laid out on a variant of the cross shape usual for a major church, with the most sacred areas towards the east.

The eastern end of the church was eight bays long, with an aisle on each side flanking all but the two easternmost bays. In most churches of this plan, the high altar would be the focal point, situated in the presbytery to the east of the aisles. Because St Andrews was a major shrine, the far east end was probably a relic chapel where St Andrew's relics were kept. The presbytery was to the west of this.

Further west were the bishop's cathedra, or throne, and the canons' choir. The choir stalls extended down both sides of the presbytery towards the pulpitum, a screen separating the choir from the nave. It filled the whole of the eastern bay of the nave, a gift from William Bower, the parish vicar, in the early 1400s.

The east end of the church was a favoured place of burial for bishops and archbishops. Bishop Henry Wardlaw, in whose time St Andrews University was founded, was interred on the north side of the presbytery in 1440. Fragments from his stone effigy and tomb are on display in the cathedral museum. The entire cathedral was badly damaged by fire in 1378, and some of the repairs subsequently carried out can still be seen. These include replacing the windows in the upper tiers of the east gable with a single large window, and raising the presbytery floor to create an elevated relic chamber. The large grave-slab in the presbytery marks the height of the raised floor level. This has been moved slightly to reveal three stone sarcophagi, or coffins, all now empty.

Projecting from either side of the choir were transepts, or cross arms, each of four bays. Both had an aisle of three chapels on the east side, each with its own altar. These chapels supplemented the high altar. Two more in the side aisles were used for more private acts of devotion.

In the SW corner of the south transept is the night stair. This gave the canons direct access from the dormitory into the church for their night office.

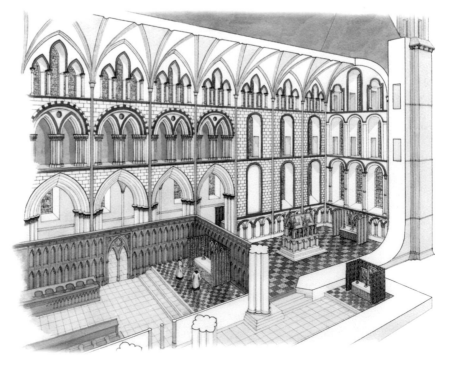

Opposite: The choir and presbytery, with the east gable beyond. St Rule's is to the right.

Right: Inside the east end of the cathedral before the rebuilding work of the late 14th century, when the upper tiers of windows in the east gable were replaced with a single large window.

THE CATHEDRAL PRIORY

The main living quarters of the Augustinian canons who maintained the cathedral's services were arranged around a cloister quadrangle to the south of the church.

Beyond lay the many other buildings required by such a wealthy institution – an infirmary for sick and elderly canons, the prior's residence, guest halls, granaries and so on. There were also other churches, including the old burgh church of Holy Trinity which stood to the east of the cathedral and was used by local people until it was replaced by a new building on South Street in 1412.

Above: The spacious interior of the chapter house as it may have looked after it was rebuilt in the early 1300s.

Opposite top: The surviving west tower viewed from the south transept, where some finely carved arches have survived.

Opposite bottom left: Stone coffins uncovered beneath the chapter house floor, where priors, patrons and other people of high status were buried.

Opposite bottom right: The paved section was a slype or passageway leading between the cathedral's south transept and the chapter house into the cloister.

Throughout the Middle Ages there was continual building, alteration and rebuilding. Surviving records show that the dormitory, dining hall and guest hall were completed during Prior John White's time (1236–58) and that Prior John of Haddington added a hall to his residence in about 1270. Bishop William Lamberton rebuilt the chapter house in time for the burial of Prior John of Forfar in 1321. This and other building operations may have been necessitated by the destruction caused during the Wars of Independence. Other alterations were made because of changes of fashion, pious benefactions or patrons' wishes to leave their mark on the building.

The priory buildings largely survive as foundations only, but their layout is still discernible. Lord Bute rebuilt some of the buildings in the 1890s. These are clearly distinguished by their neat red sandstone walls.

THE WEST RANGE

The west range was put to a variety of uses through the years, but what survives dates from the 1500s. The upper floor may have been the residence of the sub-prior. At a later date, the senzie house was here, a consistory court where church authorities heard legal cases which fell within their jurisdiction. The elaborate 13th-century arcading running along the church wall where it joined the upper level of the west range marks this out as a particularly important space.

THE SOUTH RANGE

The most important building in the south range was the refectory at first-floor level. Only the extensively restored undercroft remains, now housing part of the cathedral museum. The well in the cloister walk marks the position where the canons ritually washed their hands before going in to dine.

THE EAST RANGE

The east range contained several important rooms. Next to the church was the slype, or parlour, a covered passage which led from the cloister to the buildings beyond. Conversation was permitted here. Book cupboards in the adjacent NE corner of the cloister remind us that the cloister was a place of study.

Next to the slype was the chapter house, where the business of the priory was conducted. The canons sat on stone seats along the walls, some of which survive. This was a favoured burial place for priors and patrons of the priory. Several stone coffins have been exposed beneath its floor.

The rest of the ground floor was divided into various rooms, including the warming house, where a fire allowed the canons some comfort in winter. This was partly reconstructed in the 1890s and now contains part of the cathedral museum. The dormitory was spread over the upper floor, connected to the church via the night stair. A day stair near the south end of the range led down into the cloister. To the south were the latrines, close to the canons' dormitory, but sufficiently distanced from the church.

THE GRAVEYARD

One of the cathedral's most distinctive features is its vast graveyard, which gradually covered the site in the decades following the Reformation of 1560. It continued in use well into the 20th century.

The majority of medieval burials took place in sacred ground which had been consecrated by a bishop. There was a monastic graveyard here when the cathedral was in use, where the canons would have been buried. The ordinary people of the burgh were buried around the parish church, which was within the precinct until the early 15th century.

Medieval graveyards were used for all sorts of activities besides burials, including fairs, markets and wapinschawings, at which men were drilled in combat techniques, so this was not always the most peaceful of resting places. Burials were frequently moved or cut by new interments and disturbed bones were stored elsewhere to make space for new burials. Churchyards became raised and uneven as more earth was added and new burials were inserted.

After the Reformation, it was no longer necessary for ground to be consecrated before it was used for burials, which meant that land other than the churchyards could be used. As the population grew and commemoration became more affordable, gravestones proliferated.

Ordinary people increasingly wanted their own burial plots and to be able to visit the graves of their relatives. Overcrowded town churchyards were not desirable final resting places. Open spaces on the edges of towns such as St Andrews Cathedral precinct were reused as graveyards.

Examples of grave-slabs and memorials from various periods are on display in the cathedral museum, indicating the number and diversity of burials that took place here. To this day, many people visit the cathedral in search of the graves of their forebears.

Above: The abundance of gravestones around St Rule's demonstrates the use of the cathedral grounds as a burial place after the Reformation.

Left: The grave of the famous golfer 'Tommy' Morris Jnr, or 'Young Tom Morris', who was born in St Andrews and died here in 1875, aged just 24. He won the British Open at 17, a record which still stands.

THE CATHEDRAL MUSEUM

The museum is housed in three rooms on either side of the visitor reception: these include the restored warming house and the refectory undercroft. Between them, they house a collection of artefacts discovered around the cathedral over the past 200 years.

ST ANDREWS SARCOPHAGUS

In 1833, fragments of sculptured stone were found during gravedigging near St Rule's. These appeared to be part of a sarcophagus – a container for a body (literally, a 'flesh eater'). The St Andrews Sarcophagus, as it has come to be known, is one of the finest pieces of sculpture to survive from early-medieval Europe.

Detailed research has concluded that the 'sarcophagus' is in fact a royal burial shrine of the late 700s. It may have been built over a king's grave; or it could have contained saintly relics. Possibly, the shrine was a memorial to Onuist son of Uurguist (died 761), a king from a powerful Pictish dynasty. An alternative interpretation is that this is part of a stone screen. Whatever its function, this is the key evidence for one of the churches which stood here on the headland at this early date.

The largest surviving panel depicts a busy scene including human and animal figures. At the centre top, a mounted Pictish king attacks a lion. To his right, the biblical King David is shown rending the

jaws of a lion – a motif that appears elsewhere in Pictish carving. The message is that heavenly salvation is obtainable through the righteous behaviour of strong kings who defend the Christian faith. It is thought that the shrine stood in a church near the altar. The design provides an insight into the religious beliefs, political aspirations and international contacts of the Pictish kings. Its sculptor clearly had access to artistic models derived from elsewhere. The shoes, weapons and horse gear of the rider are all typically Pictish, but his clothes are Byzantine in style and the ornate knife scabbard is modelled on contemporary Germanic types. Carved in high relief, the figures almost walk off the panels, resembling early-Christian carvings in ivory from the eastern Mediterranean.

Top right: The interior of the refectory undercroft, housing part of the museum.

Right: The main panel of the Sarcophagus.

THE CATHEDRAL MUSEUM (CONTINUED)

EARLY-MEDIEVAL STONES

St Leonard's school shrine

This house-shaped shrine dates from the 800s and would originally have stood over an individual grave. It was discovered in 1895 among burial cists during building work SW of the cathedral. The early monastery may have had several burial grounds, perhaps associated with the seven churches mentioned in the foundation legend. A fragment of a similar shrine was discovered at St Vigeans, near Arbroath, and is on display at the museum there.

High crosses

Free-standing high crosses were elaborately carved stones, usually over 4m high. They would have stood at strategic points in the monastic complex. Decorated with a mix of abstract art and biblical scenes, they could be described as sermons in stone.

Cross-slabs

Most of the early medieval stones are cross-slabs. The Picts became Christian before AD 700 and were soon incorporating Christian symbols into their art. Stone slabs with the cross as the central motif appeared all over Pictland. There are similarities between Pictish cross-slabs and the illuminated gospel books being produced in Anglo-Saxon Northumbria and Gaelic Iona. This suggests close cultural ties between the regions.

SEALS

Also displayed in the museum is a collection of casts made from seals associated with the bishops and archbishops of St Andrews. The originals date from the 1100s to the 1500s and are held in various archives.

In the medieval period, sealing a document was the normal process by which it was authenticated. The seal also closed a document to keep its contents private. Engraved metal seal matrixes or dies were used to create impressions in hot wax, and these were carefully curated to prevent their loss, breakage or fraudulent use. Generally speaking, the size of a seal was an indication of the importance of the owner. The seals of bishops show them in their full regalia and later examples include canopies, saints, arms and detailing.

STONES FROM THE CATHEDRAL

After the Reformation, the statues and other carved stones of the cathedral were torn down or defaced by Reformers. Others were carried off for use elsewhere in the town. During the 19th century, more stones were uncovered, including some exceptional examples of the stone-carver's art.

POST-REFORMATION STONES

St Andrews Cathedral has one of the finest collections of post-Reformation gravestones in Scotland. Dating mainly from the 1600s, they contain a wealth of information about the more affluent citizens of St Andrews, their spouses and offspring. The stones record the names of the deceased, their age and date of death, sometimes in English, sometimes Latin. Many offer a thought-provoking epithet. Emblems of mortality abound, including skulls, crossbones and grave-diggers' tools.

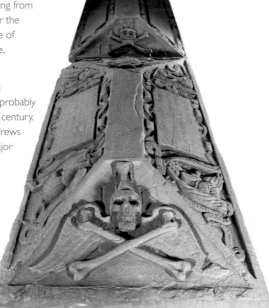

Opposite top:
A 'house shrine' dating from the 800s, found near the cathedral on the site of St Leonard's College, now a school.

Opposite centre:
A Pictish cross-slab probably dating from the 9th century. At that time, St Andrews was the site of a major early-Christian settlement known as Cennrígmonaid (Kilrymont).

Right:
An elaborate 17th-century gravestone with skull and crossbones.

Opposite bottom left:
Seals of Bishop James Kennedy (1440–65) and of the chapter, or governing body, of the cathedral (1200s).

A MASON'S SKETCH

These markings, discovered on the underside of a pillar fragment, give us a direct insight into the building practices of the early 1200s. The carefully drawn and scribed lines show the plan of a wall with a three-lobed attached column. There are also four neat circles, created using a compass, which could be plans for the small columns which still exist on the upper surface of the base.

These are the preserved notes of a medieval stonemason – working drawings from a time before professional architects, when masons were responsible for designing buildings. Only three other examples of masons' plans are known in Scotland – at Dunfermline Abbey, Torphichen Preceptory and Rosslyn Chapel.

Medieval master masons were wealthy and respected individuals, men of great skill who designed incredible buildings with the simplest of tools. Most masons were 'journeymen', who travelled between jobs. These men marked their handiwork with 'signature' symbols so that it could be checked and attributed to them. Masons' marks can be seen carved into stones around the cathedral.

THE PRECINCT WALL AND THE PENDS GATE

The wall which surrounded the cathedral precinct marked the boundary between the sacred space of the Church and the secular world beyond.

St Andrews precinct wall is now the most complete in Scotland. The surviving section begins at the NE corner of the cathedral, and swings around the east and south sides to a section on the SW side which has been re-aligned in recent times. Of the original 16 towers, 13 survive – two rectangular, the rest circular – as well as four gateways.

The principal entrance was the 14th-century Pends Gate, which stands immediately west of the cathedral, spanning the modern road which bears its name. The Teinds Gate, on Abbey Walk, is where the canons received their dues from the parish. This amounted to one-tenth of its annual produce from land and labour and was the main source of income for the priory. This produce was stored in a nearby teinds barn. The Mill Port, or Sea Yett, leads to the harbour.

The upper parts of the precinct wall date to the time of Prior John Hepburn (died 1526) and his nephew Patrick, who succeeded him. Prior John's coat of arms is displayed on the towers and gates.

The Pends Gate has fine blind arches above its entrance. These are similar to the ones designed for the cathedral's west front after the fire of 1378. Great timber gates were installed one bay into the pend. These were opened to allow foot traffic and wheeled transport to enter the precinct though their respective openings.

Above: The arms of Prior John Hepburn (including his initials IH) as preserved in the cathedral museum. Similar painted armorials would have been displayed at points along the precinct wall.

Right: The Pends Gate, at the west of the cathedral precinct.

Top right: Part of the precinct wall.

Above: The cathedral and precinct as they may have looked around 1550, showing the full extent of the precinct wall.

Continue SE, through the Sea Yett to the harbour.
Although it is too cramped for trading, fishing has been
a staple industry here at least since the early 13th century.
Follow the walls past the boats up to the clifftop ruins.

ST MARY'S CHURCH, KIRKHEUGH

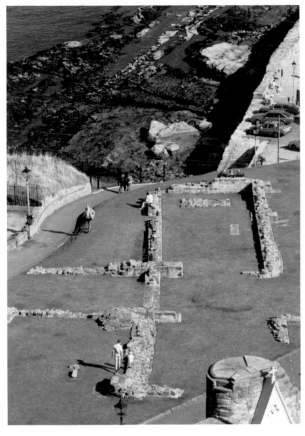

Above: Although little survives of St Mary's, its cross-shaped layout is clearly visible.

Below: The seal of St Mary's monastic chapter.

The site of St Mary's Church has been part of the monastic complex from the very beginning. It became the home of the Culdees – the Celtic monks supplanted from the cathedral by the Augustinians in the 1120s.

The ruins of St Mary's Church perch on the cliff-edge to the NE of the cathedral. Although the building survives only as wall-footings, the cross shape of the church is clearly marked out. Some of the early-medieval cross-slabs now on display in the cathedral museum were found here in 1860, during the construction of a coastal defence battery.

St Mary's was given to the Culdee monks who refused to join the new Augustinian cathedral priory, established around 1123. In 1248–9 their successors became Scotland's first college of secular priests. These priests did not take vows and lived a less enclosed life than their monastic neighbours, the Augustinian canons 'regular'.

The Culdees' college was a place of learning and it enjoyed the patronage of kings and bishops. However, the Augustinian canons may have been less pleased with its status, regarding it as a rival establishment. By the time of the Reformation in 1560, there were at least 13 clergy in this college, each funded by an endowment or prebend held by the college.

The earliest surviving part of the church is the nave to the west. The finest masonry is found in the choir at the east, extended at some stage to provide the clergy with more space. At the east end is the base of the high altar. A stone projection in the south wall may have supported the sedilia – seats for the officiating clergy. A door in the opposite wall probably led to the sacristy, a storage place for vestments and precious items. A small bell-tower would have crowned the centre of the church. To the SE is a reconstructed wall, which may have been part of the accommodation for the clergy.

ST ANDREW AND ST RULE

According to Scripture, St Andrew was a Galilean fisherman and disciple of Christ. A tradition later grew up that he had been crucified on an X-shaped cross or saltire. He seems to have replaced St Columba as national patron saint by about 1100s Andrew and his saltire became symbols of great religious and political power, and the Scots believed that this most powerful saint had chosen to protect them.

St Rule (or Regulus) is traditionally believed to have been the guardian of St Andrew's relics. The story goes that Rule resolved to remove the relics from Patras in Greece in AD 345, following a visit from an angel who told him that they should be taken to Constantinople. He decided to take them elsewhere and his boat was ultimately wrecked off the Fife coast.

The sacred bones of St Andrew were brought here and interred in a shrine. This version of the story was written down in the 1100s around the time that the Augustinian community was settling here.

In the Middle Ages, the relics of St Andrew were distributed around Europe. (He is patron saint of numerous countries, including Greece, Romania, Russia, Ukraine and the Philippines.) The Scottish church claimed to have three fingers of his right hand, a part of one arm, a kneecap and a tooth. Possession of such important relics placed St Andrews on a par with the great shrine of St James at Santiago de Compostela in Spain. If St Andrews had such relics, it is possible that they were brought here in the 700s from Northumbria, where worship of St Andrew was strong.

Above: The martyrdom of St Andrew as depicted on a 15th-century manuscript.

THE HISTORIC BURGH

collegium S. Saluatoris

Ecclesia S Saluatoris

Franciscanorum ædes.

Dominicanorum ædes.

domus vrbis

Ecclesia Perochiæ ciuitatis.

collegium D. Mariani

Arx Episcopi.

Collegium D Leonardi

Students, golfers and tourists travelling the picturesque road alongside the Eden Estuary to the ancient university town of St Andrews could be forgiven for believing they were approaching a remote place, hemmed by dunes, salt marshes and farmland.

Yet for hundreds of years St Andrews played a central role in Scottish religion and politics. A prosperous burgh grew up alongside the cathedral and castle, swelled by pilgrims visiting the shrine of St Andrew.

The layout of the medieval town is preserved in its street plan, wonderfully depicted on this map produced by John Geddy around 1580. This rare survival shows all the medieval monuments, as well as familiar features of a medieval town, such as the market cross, tron (town scales) and burgage plots.

MARKET STREET AND NORTH STREET

Turn right up **City Road** to the west end of **Market Street.** At this point you may wish to visit **St Andrews Museum,** whose collection explores the town's history from medieval times to the present. If so, turn left into **Kinburn Park. The tour continues on Market Street.**

The site of another town gate is marked on the pavement at the west end of Market Street. A little to its east, where the cobbles end, is the site of the *domus urbis* (town house) or tolbooth. This was the administrative heart of medieval St Andrews. It functioned as a burgh court, prison and treasury. Taxes gathered at the town ports were stored here, as were the town weights and measures. St Andrews retained its medieval tolbooth until 1862.

A little further up Market Street, on your left, is Greyfriars Gardens, named for the Franciscan community whose church once stood here. Carved stones from the friary were found in 1881 when a well was cleared.

Further still up Market Street is the Whyte-Melville Memorial Fountain. This was erected in 1880 in memory of Victorian novelist George Whyte-Melville. Market Street was also the site of the market cross and the tron, the town's weighing machine.

Top left: The 15th-century church and tower of St Salvator's College.

Far left: A photograph of the tolbooth before its demolition in 1862.

Left: The initials PH commemorate the martyrdom of the Protestant preacher Patrick Hamilton in 1528.

Turn left into another vennel, Muttoes Lane. On reaching North Street, you will see St Salvator's tower to your right.

St Salvator's is the oldest of the university's three medieval colleges. However, the church is all that remains of the original building. It was founded in 1450 by Bishop Kennedy, whose impressive monument survives inside. His tomb and gilded silver mace are reminders of the incredible wealth and resources commanded by Scotland's medieval bishops. North of the church, ranges of buildings were arranged around a quadrangle. The medieval buildings were replaced in the 1800s.

The survival of the chapel is miraculous, given its turbulent history. Outside the tower, the initials 'PH' are marked out in cobbles, on the spot where the Protestant martyr Patrick Hamilton was burned at the stake in 1528. The grand interior furnishings of the chapel were later damaged by Reformers.

Tucked into the SE corner of St Salvator's College, 71 North Street was built by Patrick Adamson before he became archbishop in 1575. Note the gunholes in the tower.

From St Salvator's turn left towards Golf Place, at the west end of North Street.

On Golf Place stands the clubhouse of the Royal and Ancient Golf Club. This imposing Victorian edifice, built in 1853–4, is an important landmark in the recent history of St Andrews as a centre of golf. Founded in 1754, the club continues to thrive, with around 2,400 members throughout the world.

In recent times, its role as the governing body of golf has been taken over by a separate entity called the R&A, also based in St Andrews. The R&A organises many important matches including the Open Championship.

The Old Course, in use for over 500 years, opens up in front of the clubhouse, hemmed by the natural beauty of the West Sands, a popular place for walking and kite-surfing. The more leisurely attractions of the British Golf Museum and St Andrews Aquarium (with its resident common seals) are situated nearby.

Right: The gilded silver mace of Bishop James Kennedy, founder of St Salvator's, now held at the university museum.

THE HISTORY OF ST ANDREWS

For over 1,200 years, St Andrews has held a special status in the minds of the people of Scotland. In medieval times, this was the seat of Scotland's Church, the shrine of its national saint and as a result fabulously wealthy and influential. Even today, its ruins have a striking grandeur.

The relationship between the burgh and its great cathedral meant that the town's fall from grace after the Reformation of 1560 was dramatic. Ironically, the town's stagnation following the demise of Catholicism in Scotland helped to save its great monuments from demolition and redevelopment. The buildings of St Andrews continued to fascinate visitors, such as the travel writer Thomas Pennant, whose *Tour of Scotland* (1772) expresses awe at 'the magnificent, the pious works of past generations'.

Golf was the unlikely saviour of the town in the 19th century. Today it has risen to importance again – as an international focus for golf and a noted university town, with a thriving tourist trade appreciative of its unique cultural heritage.

THE EARLY CHURCH

In the early-medieval period, St Andrews was known as Kilrymont, which means 'church on the head of the king's mount'. This spelling derives from the earlier Pictish form, Cennrígmonaid.

The earliest reference to the settlement's existence is from 747, when Irish annals record the death of an abbot, Túathalán. This unique reference to a distant Pictish religious house in an Irish source attests to the early importance of Kilrymont as a church centre. The monastic community was probably founded by a Pictish king and there may well have been a royal residence somewhere in the vicinity. The brethren were then the *céli Dé* (Culdees). These were a group of clergy living a communal life dedicated to worship, whose spiritual life was derived from Irish monasticism.

The existence of an early monastic community here is confirmed by surviving sculpture, including the St Andrews Sarcophagus (see page 35). All of the early-medieval sculpture was found within an area of 10 acres (4.05 ha), in the NE corner of the cathedral precinct. This probably represents the limits of the early medieval monastic precinct.

One version of the foundation legend for the church at Kilrymont states that the boundary of the Pictish monastery was defined by free-standing crosses. Seven fragments from crosses of this kind were incorporated into the west face of the east gable. Their presence in this important location suggests a desire to emphasise continuity between the new cathedral and earlier religious establishments on the site. The fragments are now on display in the cathedral museum. Within the boundary there are said to have been seven churches, but the principal church was probably on the headland above the harbour, later the location of St Mary's, Kirkheugh, used by the Culdee community after the foundation of the cathedral.

The most famous foundation legend for St Andrews states that the saint's relics were brought here from Greece in the 4th century by St Rule. However, this story was not popularised until the 12th century and precisely when the relics reached Kilrymont is not known. At the time when Kilrymont became prominent, Columba was the pre-eminent saint of the Celtic Church. In 849 Cináed son of Alpin (Kenneth mac Alpin), king of the Gaels in the west and the Picts in the east, moved some of St Columba's relics from Iona to Dunkeld, Perthshire. Dunkeld became the first centre of the post-Columban church in Pictland. However, the importance of Kilrymont was soon to assert itself.

Left: Part of a cross-head dating from Pictish times, now displayed in the cathedral museum.

The strength of the settlement's royal connections was demonstrated in 943 when King Constantín son of Aed abdicated his throne in order to lead the monastic community here. At this time, the church was dominated by such monastic leaders. Elsewhere in Europe, the church was more commonly led by bishops responsible for defined geographical areas, known as dioceses. But we know that from the 10th century there were chief bishops of the Scots, some of whom were probably based at Kilrymont.

Left: Two Pictish cross-shafts, now in the cathedral museum.

Above: A Pictish holy man or pilgrim depicted on a cross-slab at St Vigeans, about 20 miles (30km) NE of St Andrews.

TIMELINE

AROUND 750	943

ONUIST SON OF UURGUIST
King of Picts, reputedly re-founds a church at Kilrymont. The Sarcophagus (left) may be his memorial.

CONSTANTÍN SON OF AED
King of Picts and Gaels, abdicates, possibly under duress, to take up a monastic life at Kilrymont.

A BISHOP'S SEAT

By the mid-900s, the title of abbot of Kilrymont had disappeared. The post seems to have been absorbed into the role of the bishop of St Andrews.

Although it is known that some of the early bishops visited Rome, religious practice in Scotland's 'Celtic' churches was different from that of the Romish church which dominated the rest of Europe. This began to change around 1070, when Malcolm III married the Saxon princess, Margaret, at Dunfermline. Malcolm's deeply religious queen resolved to bring the Scottish Church into line with the rest of Europe. She founded a Benedictine community at Dunfermline, and showed her devotion to St Andrew by providing a ferry over the River Forth, the Queen's Ferry, for pilgrims to the saint's shrine.

KING MALCVM CAMNOIR MARIIT SANCT
MERGRET OF DVNFERMLIN QVHA BVRE TO HIM
ANE SONE CALLIT EDVERO QVHILK SVCCEDIT TO
THE CROVN AND DEIT V OVT SVCCESSIOVN
GOTTIN OF HIS BODY AND EFTER SVCCEDIT
TO HIM KING ROBERT BRVCE NERREST TO
YE SAID EDVERD OF BLVDE

AN AUGUSTINIAN CHAPTER

Margaret's fifth son, Alexander I (1107–24) made three attempts to appoint bishops to Kilrymont to help him reform the church. The first two proved unsuccessful. The third was Robert, Prior of Scone, near Perth. Robert resolved to introduce a community of Augustinian canons to make Kilrymont a model cathedral foundation. As the cathedral chapter, they would be responsible for electing and advising bishops and for providing services within the cathedral.

When Robert became bishop in 1123, there were at least two groups of Culdees at Kilrymont. Neither group accepted responsibility for the main services in the cathedral; moreover both groups appear to have included married men. Neither can have been viewed with favour by a reforming bishop.

Top: The seal of Abel de Golin, who was briefly bishop of St Andrews in 1254.

Left: King Malcolm III and his wife Queen Margaret (later St Margaret), who founded the Queen's Ferry across the Firth of Forth to assist pilgrims wishing to visit St Andrews.

Bishop Robert was determined that both groups would be superseded by Augustinian canons, but that the Culdees should be given the opportunity to become canons. In the event they preferred to remain as a separate body and were eventually given a permanent home in St Mary's Church, Kirkheugh. In 1248 Bishop David de Bernham constituted them as a college of secular priests and thereafter they seem to have served as almost a rival cathedral chapter (see page 40).

As the Culdee community faded into the background, so too did the Celtic place name Kilrymont. The name St Andrews came to be applied to Bishop Robert's new cathedral priory and to the town in its shadow. This is first mentioned in a charter of Bishop Roger in 1189 which refers to the relocation of the market cross.

No archaeological investigation has yet clarified the location of the original settlement. However, the parish church of Holy Trinity was situated in the priory precinct until 1412, which implies a close relationship between the secular and religious settlements from an early date. It has been suggested that North and South Castle Street might have been the main axis of early settlement.

Left: Augustinian canons share a frugal meal in silence while listening to a reading from scripture.

AROUND 1070

PRINCESS MARGARET
marries King Malcolm III.
She soon establishes a ferry north of Edinburgh to assist pilgrims on their way to St Andrews.

1123

ROBERT, PRIOR OF SCONE
is appointed bishop of St Andrews and establishes an Augustinian house here.

BUILDING SCOTLAND'S GREATEST CHURCH

The cathedral at St Andrews was the church within which Scotland's most important bishop had his cathedra (throne). It was the mother church of the bishop's diocese as well as a major place of pilgrimage.

Around 1140, King David I gave permission for the founding of an ecclesiastical burgh at St Andrews. This was a turning-point. When the vast new church was begun in the 1160s, the scale of cathedrals throughout Scotland began to change.

The cathedral was begun on the orders of Bishop Arnold, who died a few months before construction began in 1163. It took well over a century to complete. Indeed, as with many great cathedrals, building works were probably in progress throughout most of its existence. Some were prompted by changes in liturgical or architectural fashion, others by structural damage.

Even as the masons were completing the west end of the nave in the 1270s, a great gale blew it down. A century later, in 1378, a devastating fire raged through the building. Rebuilding suffered yet another setback in 1409, when the gable of the south transept was blown down in another storm, damaging both the church and the adjacent priory buildings.

The completed cathedral was an immense cross-shaped building, 109m long. It had a nave of twelve bays with aisles on both sides, a massive central tower, twin transepts with three chapels each and a six-bay choir, again with an aisle on each side. Beyond the high altar at the east end was a relic chapel, where St Andrew's relics were kept. Despite its extended construction and many changes in design, the finished cathedral appeared strikingly uniform. Its great scale would have immediately struck pilgrims approaching from the sea or along the converging streets of the town.

As well as a national shrine and centre of the Scottish Church, the cathedral was the everyday home of its chapter, the Augustinian canons who undertook the daily round of services and prayer. They lived in the priory to the south of the church, which was an integral part of the cathedral design. Like the cathedral church itself, the priory buildings were subject to constant change. They were still not complete at the time of the cathedral's consecration in 1318.

Prior William of Lothian (1340–54) 'covered the whole dormitory with a handsome roof of timber below and of lead above; he also roofed the old church, the east chamber, and four parts of the cloister and many other buildings'. This structure survived until 1378, when it was damaged by the great fire.

Right: This grave-cover, on display in the cathedral museum, is a rare depiction of a medieval stonemason. He lies flanked by his tools: a set square and a hammer.

PILGRIMAGE

The shrine of St Andrew was one of the most important pilgrimage places in western Christendom. Aside from Santiago de Compostela in Spain, it was unique in offering pilgrims contact with a martyred first-chosen disciple of Christ.

Up to the Reformation, many thousands of pilgrims came to St Andrews, seeking a cure for ailments or remission from sin. The earliest recorded pilgrim is an Irish prince in 967. In 1512, a foundation charter converted St Leonard's Hospital into a college of the university.

Right: A pilgrim badge dating from the 1300s, depicting St Andrew. It would have been sewn to clothing or a hat using four stitching holes, of which only one survives. It was cast from an alloy of tin and lead.

Far right: Medieval pilgrims arriving at St Andrews.

DID YOU KNOW . . .

When medieval pilgrims travelled to shrines, they did so in search of salvation, often returning with souvenirs. These allowed the powers of the saint to continue working for them or for family members. For example, visitors to the shrine of St Thomas a Beckett at Canterbury could purchase ampullae – small lead phials of holy water, allegedly mixed with the blood and brains of Beckett. Some of these have been found in Perth. Their souvenir badges were also believed to be imbued with sacred power.

Up until then, it had been the town's main hostel for pilgrims, and this may indicate a fall-off in popularity.

The relics of St Andrew were believed to be a tooth, a kneecap, three fingers and an arm-bone. They were held in a reliquary known as the *mòr breac*, perhaps a jewelled box.

This was carried in procession around the town during major festivals, which included St Andrew's Day (30 November). At all other times they were kept in the treasury at the east end of the cathedral. This would almost certainly have been a target for the Reformers who ravaged the cathedral in June 1559 (see page 69).

1160s

BISHOP ARNOLD OF ST ANDREWS begins building the great cathedral next to the existing church of St Rule's.

1270s

COMPLETION OF THE CATHEDRAL is set back when a wild storm wrecks the west end of the nave.

THE WARS OF INDEPENDENCE

In the 1290s, a crisis in Scotland's royal succession led to long and devastating conflict with England. The bishops of St Andrews had a pivotal role in determining the balance of power, and their involvement embroiled the town in some of the most important events in Scotland's medieval history.

In 1290, Bishop William Fraser of St Andrews invited Edward I of England to arbitrate between rival claimants to the Scottish throne. Presented with an opportunity to seize power, Edward installed John Balliol, lord of Galloway, as a puppet ruler and assumed for himself the title Lord Paramount of Scotland. When his authority was threatened, Edward invaded.

In 1296, Edward sacked Berwick-upon-Tweed, then Scotland's chief port, and continued north, pausing briefly at St Andrews before heading north to preside over Balliol's abdication. He next returned to the castle in early 1304 with his queen, Margaret. This time he held a parliament in the cathedral priory, at which William Wallace was declared an outlaw, before going on to besiege mighty Stirling Castle. He had the roof of St Andrews Cathedral stripped of lead, for melting down to make artillery shot.

Top left: King Robert I (the Bruce), who held his first parliament in the cathedral priory in 1309, three years after seizing the throne.

Left: The siege of Carlisle in 1315, at which a Scottish force used a trebuchet – a stone-throwing catapult. Although this siege was repelled, a similar machine known as 'the Boustour' was used successfully by Sir Andrew Murray when he besieged the English in Castle in 1337.

While at the siege of Stirling with King Edward, Bishop William Lamberton of St Andrews made a secret pact with Robert the Bruce to rise up against the English aggressor. When Bruce made his audacious bid for the throne in March 1306, Lamberton was present at Scone Abbey to celebrate pontifical High Mass for the new king. Lamberton also hosted King Robert's first parliament, held in the cathedral priory in March 1309.

The outbreak of the Wars of Independence in 1296 had prevented the consecration of the newly completed cathedral. The opportunity to redress that came after Bruce's great victory over Edward II at Bannockburn in 1314. On 5 July 1318, Lamberton presided over the consecration ceremony in the presence of King Robert himself.

Lamberton died in 1328. The death of King Robert a year later resulted in the Wars of Independence breaking out once more.

By the 1330s, the castle was once more in the hands of the English, who attempted to strengthen the defences in 1336. Their work was in vain. The following year Sir Andrew Murray, regent in the absence of King Robert I's son David II, recaptured it after a major siege lasting three weeks. Thereafter the castle was rendered indefensible so that the English could never again use it as a garrison fortress.

The 1337 siege of the castle was successful largely on account of the presence of a siege machine called 'the Boustour'. It was probably a great stone-throwing machine, called a trebuchet, not unlike a Scottish example shown in a charter of the city of Carlisle dated 1316. The Boustour was taken from St Andrews to Murray's ancestral castle, Bothwell, on the Clyde south of Glasgow, which also fell to the Scots.

Right: The seal of Bishop William Lamberton of St Andrews, a staunch supporter of King Robert against the English invaders.

DID YOU KNOW . . .

Bishop Lamberton was not alone in supporting Bruce's claim to the throne. Bishop Wishart of Glasgow was also a staunch supporter, even after Robert Bruce savagely murdered his rival John Comyn at Greyfriars Church in Dumfries. For these great men of the Scottish Church, English domination meant the subordination of the Scottish bishops to the archdiocese of York, and the bishops would accept no authority between their Church and the Pope.

1304

EDWARD I OF ENGLAND resides at St Andrews Castle and holds a parliament in the cathedral priory.

1337

SIR ANDREW MURRAY recaptures the castle for the Scots. The defences are demolished to render it useless to an English garrison.

THE TRAILL CASTLE

The devastation caused by the Wars of Independence necessitated wholesale rebuilding of the bishop's castle. The task was carried out on the orders of Bishop Walter Traill, who died within its reconstructed walls in 1401.

Much of what we can see now dates from Traill's time. The castle was protected from attack by a tall, thick curtain wall of stone with five towers, all probably square in plan, at the angles. The fore tower housed an impressive entrance protected by a drawbridge. Residential accommodation for the bishop, his large household and his guests was provided within the towers and in ranges built along the inside of the curtain wall. Further accommodation was provided in an outer courtyard to the west, similarly protected by a defensive ditch and wall.

Traill's castle was built in the age before gunpowdered artillery was a real threat. The garrison could defend the castle either from the battlements at the wall-heads or from within the towers. Wide and deep rock-cut ditches kept besiegers and their siege machines well away from the walls at a time when the effective range of a trebuchet was 200m.

Before the advent of effective artillery, siege warfare was chiefly a waiting game, with the besiegers attempting to take the castle through starvation and disease. The huge amount of storage accommodation and the well in the courtyard show the efforts made in designing the castle to equip it for a long siege.

Right: The castle around 1400, largely rebuilt by Bishop Walter Traill following the Wars of Independence. At this time there were five rectangular towers with the main entrance through the fore tower.

Below: The surviving remnants of the north range, including the sea tower (left) and the kitchen tower (right).

DID YOU KNOW ...

The main entrance to the castle was defended by a drawbridge of a type made popular by the great castle-builder, Charles V of France. Drawbridges at his castles of Bastille in Paris and nearby Vincennes had established this fashion.

THE BISHOPS AND ARCHBISHOPS OF ST ANDREWS

Maeluin	?c.1028 – 55
Tuthald	?c.1055 – 70
Fothad	c.1070 – 93
Turgot	c.1107 – 15
Queen Margaret's spiritual director and biographer	
Robert	1123 – 59
Arnold	1160 – 62
Richard	1163 – 78
John Scot	1178 – 88
Roger	1189 – 1202
William Malvoisin	1202 – 38
David de Bernham	1239 – 53
Abel de Golin	1254
Gamelin	1255 – 71
William Wishart	1271 – 79
William Fraser	1279 – 97
William Lamberton	1297 – 1328
Scottish patriot, officiated at Robert Bruce's coronation in 1306, spent two years in an English prison, but returned to oversee the completion of St Andrews Cathedral in 1318	
James Ben	1328 – 32
William Landalis	1342 – 85
Walter Traill	1385 – 1401
rebuilt the castle in the 1390s	
Henry Wardlaw	1403 – 40
founder and first chancellor of St Andrews University in 1410	
James Kennedy	1440 – 65
founder of St Salvator's College in 1450	

Patrick Graham	1465 – 78
created first archbishop in 1474; later declared insane	
William Scheves	1478 – 97
James Stewart	1497 – 1504
Alexander Stewart	1504 – 13
an illegitimate son of James IV, killed alongside his father at the Battle of Flodden	
Andrew Forman	1514 – 21
James Beaton	1521 – 39
David Beaton	1539 – 46
murdered by Fife Protestants after he had George Wishart burned at the stake	
John Hamilton	1546 – 71
hanged for murder in 1571	
John Douglas	1571 – 74
Patrick Adamson	1575 – 92
Episcopacy abolished in 1592 but revived in 1610	
George Gledstanes	1610 – 15
John Spottiswood	1615 – 38
Episcopacy abolished in 1638 but revived in 1661	
James Sharp	1661 – 79
murdered by Covenanters near St Andrews	
Alexander Burnet	1679 – 84
Arthur Ross	1684 – 89
Episcopacy finally abolished 1689	

1385

WALTER TRAILL
becomes bishop of St Andrews. He sets about rebuilding the castle, whose basic layout changes little thereafter.

1401

BISHOP TRAILL
dies within his new castle and is buried in his cathedral.

LIFE IN THE BISHOP'S HOUSEHOLD

Even when the bishop was not in residence, his castle must have been a hive of activity as the main base of the household of the country's leading churchman. When the bishop was here it was often the setting for major functions.

Most of the great figures in society set foot in the castle's courtyard. One example is James I (1406–37), who received part of his education from Bishop Henry Wardlaw, founder of St Andrews University. James I also spent Christmas here in 1425 'and kept the festivities going' until the Feast of Epiphany (6 January). He was joined by Philip of Burgundy's ambassadors and 'nearly all the princes and magnates of the kingdom'. James II's son, James III, was probably born in the castle in 1452.

A medieval lord was expected to administer local law and order and his castle had to include prison cells. St Andrews Castle was no exception.

The majority of prisoners brought here were local miscreants falling under the jurisdiction of the bishop. These were held in the castle's prison and bottle dungeon pending trial and sentencing in the castle's great hall.

The castle was also used as a state prison, and numerous important figures were confined here. David, Duke of Rothesay, eldest son and heir of King Robert III (1390–1406) was imprisoned here in 1402 on the orders of his uncle, the Duke of Albany. In 1425, Albany's own son, Duke Murdoch, was held here before his execution at Stirling Castle. Ironically, the first archbishop of St Andrews, Patrick Graham, was imprisoned in his own castle after he was deemed insane and deprived of office in 1478. Such prisoners were held not in the dungeon, but in a manner appropriate to their social standing. The upper floors of the sea tower may have been where these prisoners were 'closely warded'.

Top: The castle courtyard around 1555. By this time the main entrance had been moved to its present position (far right), with accommodation for the archbishop above.

THE CARDINAL'S HOUSEHOLD

The household serving Cardinal Beaton (see pages 66–7) was huge. His nephew, John Beaton of Balfour, constable, commanded a small army of guards, men-at-arms and gunners. Another nephew, John Lauder, was one of his secretaries. The other was Andrew Oliphant, the cardinal's 'well belovit clerk'. Two chaplains looked after his private chapel, and two almoners attended to the needy at the castle gate. His master of works had charge of the stonemasons, barrowmen, smiths and wrights working on upgrading the defences. His master of the household managed a large team of cooks and scullions. His master of the horse managed the stable hands, farriers, carters and messengers. There were also minstrels, upholsterers, gardeners and tailors. Most remain nameless, but we do know that Beaton's porter, killed on the same day as his master, was Brose Stirling. His cook, Gabriel, and his barber, Claud, were both French; and his fool's name was John Lowys.

DID YOU KNOW...

The bishops and archbishops of St Andrews had other residences, including castles at Monimail and Dairsie, both also in Fife, and a townhouse in Edinburgh. This 19th-century illustration shows Cardinal Beaton's house at Blackfriars Wynd, Edinburgh.

1412

BISHOP HENRY WARDLAW founds a university at St Andrews, the first in Scotland.

1425

KING JAMES I celebrates Christmas at St Andrews, and prolongs the festivities until the feast of Epiphany (6 January).

A CATHEDRAL CITY

St Andrews was planned around its cathedral. When the ecclesiastical burgh was founded in 1140, a Flemish town-planner known as Mainard was brought in to lay out the new settlement. His scheme was designed to throw focus on the church at its east end.

Of the three main streets, only one – Market Street – does not lead directly to the cathedral. Archaeological investigations have called into question whether this street was part of Mainard's plan. It is possible that the buildings at its east end, blocking the view of the cathedral, fill an area which was originally an open market, but this has not been proven.

Market Street was the location of the mercat cross, where the burgh market was held. Goods could be sold on most days of the week, but market days must have been particularly frenetic, as people brought animals, crops and other goods into town to be sold.

Aside from the West Port (see page 45), the burgh had several other entrances, each secured by a gate. The foundation of the burgh promoted a sense of community among the inhabitants. After a year and a day of residence, adult males could become burgesses and so enjoy the full privileges of citizenship, enabling them to participate in the political life of the town.

Above: An aerial view of the town from the west, with North Street and South Street converging on the cathedral.

Immigrants who lacked the means to purchase a plot could become labourers or servants, living in small buildings in the burgh backlands.

Among the residences and businesses of the citizens of St Andrews were hospitals, hostels and churches which catered for the many pilgrims who came to visit the shrine of St Andrew.

An important burgh such as St Andrews usually had several chapels, churches and monastic communities. Churches within the cathedral precinct included St Mary Magdalene and Holy Trinity in addition to St Rule's and the cathedral. St Peter's chapel is believed to have stood on the site of 3 North Street. St Nicholas' Hospital housed lepers well away from the townspeople, on the site now occupied by East Sands Leisure Centre.

There were also at least two friaries. The Franciscans, or 'Grey Friars' founded theirs in 1463; and the Dominicans, or 'Black Friars' in 1464.

The Church dominated the daily routine of the town's residents. The tolling of the bells marked the beginning of the working day and the closing of the gates at curfew. The liturgical year punctuated the secular life. Holy days were occasions for veneration and procession, as well as affirming the hierarchy of residents within the town. From birth to death, the Church was a common focus for all residents of St Andrews, many of whom are buried beneath the modern paving around the 19th century successor of the Holy Trinity parish church.

Education was another area dominated by the Church. As the centre of Christianity in Scotland, St Andrews was established as a place of great learning. It was therefore an obvious choice for the foundation of a university. St Andrews University, the oldest in Scotland, was formally founded in 1412 by Bishop Henry Wardlaw.

At first, the university lacked buildings, but by the time of the Reformation three colleges had been established – St Salvator's (1450), St Leonard's (1512) and St Mary's (1547). The university is perhaps the greatest legacy left by the bishops and archbishops of St Andrews, and remains central to the life of St Andrews to this day.

Left: The Sea Yett, leading from the cathedral precinct out to the harbour.

1450

ST SALVATOR'S COLLEGE
is founded, the first of three residential colleges associated with the university.

1472

BISHOP PATRICK GRAHAM
becomes Scotland's first archbishop.

JAMES BEATON STRENGTHENS THE CASTLE

In 1513, the disastrous Battle of Flodden robbed Scotland of its king and many of its leading nobles. These included the young archbishop of St Andrews. From the resulting power vacuum emerged a tough new leader for Scotland's Church.

In the early 1500s, both Scotland and England had strong and ambitious kings. In 1513, Henry VIII of England invaded France. James IV of Scotland had sought peace, but was compelled to honour Scotland's longstanding alliance with the French. When his army engaged an English force at Flodden in Northumberland, James was killed, along with many of his noblemen.

Above: The castle in the 1520s. By now circular blockhouses with coped (curved) battlements had been added at the two southern corners, each equipped with powerful artillery.

Among the dead was Archbishop Alexander Stewart of St Andrews, an illegitimate son of James IV and founder of St Leonard's College. His untimely death on the battlefield led to a scramble for the vacant see. The eventual victor was Andrew Foreman. He was succeeded in 1521 by James Beaton, then archbishop of Glasgow and lord chancellor of Scotland.

Beaton was a powerful political influence in the court of the child king James V. He urged an alliance with France to resist attempts by Henry VIII of England to gain control of Scotland. He was also a vigorous opponent of the Protestant ideas then circulating in Scotland and actively persecuted Reformers, whom he saw as heretics. Most notoriously, he was responsible for the trial and execution of the Protestant preacher Patrick Hamilton, burned at the stake outside St Salvator's College in 1528.

Beaton was probably also responsible for a building programme that greatly strengthened the defences of St Andrews Castle. The main changes were on the south and west fronts facing the land, from where the main assault would be expected. Around this time, the entrance was moved to its present position and the fore tower was redesigned to enable it to withstand attack by gunpowdered artillery, now a serious threat. The impressive drawbridge was removed in the process. The blockhouses were also added during this redevelopment (see page 17), and would have been equipped with artillery. Heavy, carriage-mounted guns were positioned at the wall-head and smaller, trestle-mounted pieces in the chambers below.

Above: A light artillery piece, of a type that would have been used on the lower floors of the blockhouses from the 1520s. It would have fired two-inch (50mm) shot and had a range of about a third of a mile (500 metres).

Far left: James IV of Scotland.

Left: His brother-in-law Henry VIII of England.

1513

ARCHBISHOP ALEXANDER STEWART of St Andrews is killed at the Battle of Flodden. His death results in a power vacuum in the Scottish Church.

1521

ARCHBISHOP JAMES BEATON of Glasgow becomes archbishop of St Andrews and head of the Scottish Church.

ST ANDREWS UNDER SIEGE

James Beaton was succeeded by his nephew David, an equally powerful figure. But the younger Beaton's persecution of Protestants would lead to calamity.

In 1537, the ageing James Beaton arranged for his nephew David to be appointed as his successor. David Beaton was an ambitious man who already held several important and lucrative church offices, including bishop of Mirepoix in France and commendator (administrator) of Arbroath Abbey. In 1538, he became archbishop of St Andrews and a cardinal of the Church – the first Scotsman in 150 years to hold the latter title.

For about a decade thereafter, Beaton was a dominant figure in Scottish politics. He made many enemies in both Scotland and Protestant England. He had strong ties to the French court, and his vehement opposition to the proposed marriage of the infant Mary Queen of Scots to Prince Edward, son and heir of Henry VIII, was a major factor leading to renewed warfare between the two countries in 1544.

> 'I am a priest. I am a priest. Fy, fy all is gone.'
>
> The last words of Cardinal Beaton, as quoted in John Knox's *Historie of the Reformatioun of Scotland.*

In March 1546, Beaton had the charismatic Protestant preacher, George Wishart, burned at the stake in front of the castle walls. By now, Protestant ideas were having a profound effect on the lives of the population, polarising Scotland's nobility. Wishart's execution was the perfect pretext for Beaton's enemies to move against him. In May of that year, a group of Fife lairds gained access to the castle by disguising themselves as stonemasons. Having overcome the garrison, the intruders seized the cardinal, stabbed him and had his naked body hung in a pair of bed sheets from the castle walls.

In an effort to remove the intruders, who were backed by the English, the castle was besieged on the orders of Regent Arran. It was at this time that the mine was dug by the besiegers and successfully intercepted by the defenders. In April 1547, during a truce, John Knox, Wishart's erstwhile sword-carrier, entered the castle. The future leader of the Protestant Reformation spoke first-hand with Beaton's murderers, and the narrative he records is biting in its condemnation of the cardinal.

Above: Cardinal David Beaton, the most powerful Scottish churchman of the 16th century.

DID YOU KNOW . . .

The French often condemned heretics to the galleys, where they suffered harsh conditions. Most lasted only a few years, but John Knox was no average oarsman. He and his fellow prisoners retained their faith, refusing to sing Salve Regina on Saturday nights. According to Knox's account, one man (possibly Knox himself) threw an image of the Virgin Mary overboard when told to kiss it.

Above: George Wishart administering holy communion at St Andrews Castle on the day of his execution, painted in 1845 by the Scottish artist Thomas Duncan.

The truce was broken when a French fleet arrived to support Regent Arran and began a devastating artillery bombardment from the sea. Guns were also fired at the castle from the towers of St Salvator's and the cathedral. The castle was soon rendered indefensible. The great hall and the eastern blockhouse were largely destroyed. Some of the rebels were imprisoned in France, while others, including Knox, became galley slaves.

Shortly before Beaton's murder, work was in hand to upgrade the fortifications. The south front was being strengthened by adding a second skin to the one built in the 1300s, as a more effective defence against bombardment.

1546

GEORGE WISHART is burned at the stake outside St Andrews Castle by Archbishop David Beaton, who is murdered soon afterward in a revenge attack.

1546

REGENT ARRAN orders a siege of the castle to remove the murderers and regain control. With French assistance, he retakes the castle by force in 1547.

ARCHBISHOP HAMILTON AND THE REFORMATION

After the dramatic events of the siege, the new archbishop set about repairing damage to the castle. But the Reformation proved an irresistible tide that would almost eradicate Catholicism in Scotland.

Cardinal Beaton was succeeded by John Hamilton, the illegitimate half-brother of Regent Arran. The thunderous artillery bombardment of 1547 had severely damaged the castle. John Knox wrote that the defences were 'razed to the ground' – though this was clearly an exaggeration. However, there was much work for Archbishop Hamilton to do.

With the east range largely destroyed, he was forced to relocate his episcopal state apartment in the south range. Much of the entrance front is his work. Hamilton's badge – a cinquefoil or five-petal flower – was liberally applied to the outer face of the new front.

Hamilton became archbishop of St Andrews in the twilight days of medieval Catholicism in Scotland. He made strenuous efforts to reform the Catholic Church from within, in an attempt to stem the tide of religious change, but his efforts were in vain. In 1560 the Reformation Parliament finally repudiated the Pope's authority in Scotland and the Catholic Mass was abolished as the main form of worship.

Above left: The new façade added to the castle entrance by Archbishop John Hamilton in the 1550s.

Left: One of the many empty statue niches at the cathedral – the result of a purge of Catholic 'idolatry' carried out by Protestant reformers.

Before then, however, much of the damage had already been done. The turning point was a sermon preached by John Knox in Holy Trinity Church on 11 June 1559. His words aroused the congregation, who were immediately moved to tear down the rich medieval furnishings associated with Catholic worship. Archbishop Hamilton seems to have bowed

to the inevitable and abandoned his great cathedral almost immediately. The roofs were stripped off and Scotland's grandest church was reduced to a stone quarry and scrap dealer's yard.

The remaining canons continued to live in the cloister, along with their master, Lord James Stewart, who was commendator and had taken over management of the cathedral. Even they were implicated in the demise of the place for in 1577 the Crown ordered them and 'all uthiris demolesaris of the cathedrall kirk thairof to desist and ceis from all forder douncasting thairof'. Even so, by the end of the century the whole complex was reportedly in a woeful state.

Hamilton fared little better than his church. He was imprisoned in 1563 for saying Mass, but was released and became an active supporter of Mary Queen of Scots. He retreated to Dumbarton Castle after her defeat at the Battle of Langside in 1568. In 1571 he was seized on a charge of involvement in two murders. The first alleged victim was Mary's husband Lord Darnley, strangled in 1567. The second was Regent Murray, who had governed Scotland after Mary's abdication in 1567 and defeated her forces at Langside, but was assassinated in 1570. Hamilton was tried and hanged at Stirling.

Above: The vandalism of the cathedral by Protestants following John Knox's notorious sermon of 11 June 1559.

1559

JOHN KNOX
preaches an inflammatory anti-Catholic sermon in Holy Trinity Church, St Andrews. The cathedral is attacked and despoiled soon afterwards.

1563

ARCHBISHOP JOHN HAMILTON
of St Andrews, having fled in 1559, is imprisoned for saying Mass. Eight years later, he is implicated in the murders of Darnley and Regent Murray and hanged.

FADING GLORIES

'Such a dreary solitude lay before us, that it informed the perfect idea of having been laid to waste by a pestilence.'

Thomas Pennant, *Tour of Scotland* (1772)

Left: The castle portrayed as a desolate ruin by John Slezer in 1693.

The Reformation proved to be a fatal blow for St Andrews Cathedral and it was never repaired. The castle was occasionally used as an episcopal residence and state prison, but by the late 1600s it too had fallen into ruin.

During the reigns of James VI and Charles I, there were times when it seemed that St Andrews would reclaim its position at the head of the Scottish Church. Both kings had lived in England since 1603 and had come to prefer the Anglican form of worship. They were also anxious to strengthen the hand of the bishops against a growing clamour for their removal. As late as 1634, Charles I called for a report on the feasibility of restoring the cathedral.

The Reformation had no immediate effect on the castle. Bishops continued to be appointed, despite the momentous religious changes. However, towards the end of the 16th century it was mainly occupied by a succession of constables on behalf of the archbishops. In 1606 Parliament decided that the castle should be separated from the archbishopric and it was granted to the Earl of Dunbar, constable since 1603. However, in 1612 the castle was returned to Archbishop Gordon Gledstanes (1604–15) who carried out repairs on the fabric.

In 1635, Charles I attempted to re-establish the estates of the archbishopric, but it was not to be. The Scottish people were not favourably disposed to a monarch whom they suspected of Popish leanings and had visited his country of birth only once since becoming king. In 1638 the Church of Scotland abolished the office of bishop and although Charles II restored it in 1661 it was finally abolished in 1689. Deprived of any function, the cathedral building fell rapidly into ruin.

The fortunes of the burgh suffered along with those of the cathedral. Trade declined and the wealthier members of society abandoned St Andrews. Even the university considered finding a new home. Visitors in the 1700s described grass-covered streets, 'filled with dunghills which are exceedingly noisome and ready to infect the air'.

Above left: King James VI, who entertained the idea of St Andrews at the head of a reformed Scottish Church, though it never came to fruition.

Above right: His son, King Charles I, who went so far as to commission a report on restoring the cathedral.

MODERN ST ANDREWS

The burgh was partly revived by an appreciation of its medieval architecture, but its recovery was cemented by the rise in popularity of its most famous sporting activity.

By the end of the 1700s, tempers had cooled sufficiently for the burgh's great medieval buildings to be appreciated once more. Repairs were undertaken to St Rule's in 1789 and in 1826 the barons of the exchequer accepted responsibility for the cathedral. In 1893 the 3rd Marquess of Bute purchased Priory House and carried out major works to the old priory buildings. His descendant, Major Michael Crichton-Stuart, entrusted them to State care in 1946.

St Andrews was revitalised by the most unlikely of saviours, the royal and ancient game of golf. Manufacture of golf balls is recorded at St Andrews in the 1700s and by the 1800s balls and clubs were made in the town and exported. Golf tourism was and remains an important contributor to the economy of the town. The sport had been played in Scotland since at least 1457, when James II saw fit to ban it, albeit temporarily. The first known club was established in Edinburgh 300 years later. In 1754, the Society of St Andrews Golfers was formed.

Today the medieval streets of St Andrews are thronged with visitors, who come to enjoy the golf, or the fine beaches and the marvellous atmosphere of this thriving university town. Of all of Scotland's ancient burghs, St Andrews has most retained its medieval heart and soul, the charm of which has ensured its future prosperity.

Top left: A party of golfers arriving in St Andrews, around 1900.

Top right: Undergraduates of the university wearing their distinctive scarlet gowns.

1689

THE OFFICE OF BISHOP is finally abolished in Scotland and the cathedral is abandoned, leaving the precinct to be used as a burial ground.

1893

THE 3RD MARQUESS OF BUTE buys the priory house, carryng out repairs to it and other priory buildings.

ARBROATH ABBEY

One of Scotland's grandest medieval abbeys, best known as the place where the famous Declaration of Arbroath was drafted in 1320.

MEIGLE MUSEUM

A superb collection of Christian carved stones found in a small Perthshire village which was once a Pictish centre of power and burial place.

ELCHO CASTLE

This attractive tower-house on the banks of the Tay is a fine example of the dynamic changes in Scottish domestic architecture of the mid-16th century.

DUNFERMLINE ABBEY AND PALACE

Founded by Malcolm III and Queen Margaret, this magnificent medieval abbey has strong connections with Scottish royalty.

	ARBROATH ABBEY	MEIGLE MUSEUM	ELCHO CASTLE	DUNFERMLINE
↗	In Arbroath town centre	In Meigle village, 6 miles SE of Glamis off the A94	5 miles SE of Perth off the A912	15 miles NW of Edinburgh off the M90
🕐	Open all year	Open summer only; other times by arrangement	Open summer only	Open all year
📞	01241 878756	01828 640612	01738 639998	01383 739026
🚗	Approx. 30 miles from St Andrews	Approx. 20 miles from St Andrews	Approx. 35 miles from St Andrews	Approx. 35 miles from St Andrews

For more information on all Historic Scotland sites, visit **www.historic-scotland.gov.uk**
To order tickets and a wide range of gifts, visit **www.historic-scotland.gov.uk/shop**

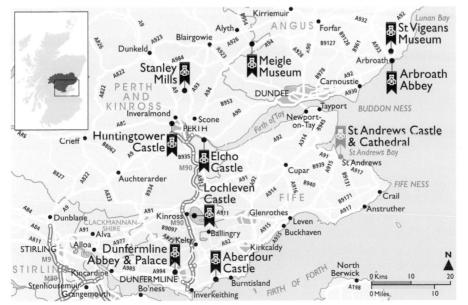

Key to facilities

Car parking	🅿
Toilets	🚻
Disabled Toilets	♿
Reasonable wheelchair access	♿
Interpretive display	
Visitor Centre	🏠
Shop	🎁
Self-serve tea and coffee	☕
Bicycle rack	🚲
Accessible by public transport	🚆
Closed lunchtime	🕐
No dogs	🚫